WORLD BOOK'S
LIBRARY OF NATURAL DISASTERS
TSUNAMIS AND SEICHES

WORLD BOOK

a Scott Fetzer company
Chicago
www.worldbookonline.com

World Book, Inc.
233 N. Michigan Avenue
Chicago, IL 60601
U.S.A.

For information about other World Book publications, visit our Web site at
http://www.worldbookonline.com or call **1-800-WORLDBK (967-5325)**.

For information about sales to schools and libraries, call **1-800-975-3250 (United States);
1-800-837-5365 (Canada)**.

Library of Congress Cataloging-in-Publication Data

Tsunamis and seiches.
       p. cm. -- (World Book's library of natural disasters)
    Summary: "A discussion of major types of natural
disasters, including descriptions of some of the most
destructive; explanations of these phenomena, what
causes them, and where they occur; and information
about how to prepare for and survive these forces of
nature. Features include an activity, glossary, list of
resources, and index"--Provided by publisher.
    Includes bibliographical references and index.
    ISBN 978-0-7166-9814-2
    1. Tsunamis--Juvenile literature.
    2. Seiches--Juvenile literature.
    I. World Book, Inc.
    GC221.5.T79 2008
    363.34'94--dc22
                      2007006185

World Book's Library of Natural Disasters
Set ISBN: 978-0-7166-9801-2

Printed in China
1 2 3 4 5 6 7 8 12 11 10 09 08 07

Editor in Chief: Paul A. Kobasa

Supplementary Publications
    Associate Director: Scott Thomas
    Managing Editor: Barbara A. Mayes

Editors: Jeff De La Rosa, Nicholas Kilzer,
    Christine Sullivan, Kristina A. Vaicikonis,
    Marty Zwikel

Researchers: Cheryl Graham, Jacqueline Jasek

Permissions Editor: Janet T. Peterson

Graphics and Design
    Associate Director: Sandra M. Dyrlund
    Associate Manager, Design: Brenda B. Tropinski
    Associate Manager, Photography: Tom Evans

Product development: Arcturus Publishing Limited

Writer: Anna Claybourne

Editors: Nicola Barber, Alex Woolf

Designer: Jane Hawkins

Illustrator: Stefan Chabluk

Acknowledgements:

Centre for Remote Imaging, Sensing and Processing, National University of Singapore and Space Imaging: 20.

Corbis: 7, 26 (Lloyd Cluff), 9, 12 (Corbis), 15 (Sergio Dorantes), 16 (Beawiharta/ Reuters), 17 (Babu/ Reuters),
    19 (Jeremy Horner), 22 (Punit Paranjpe/ Reuters), 24 (Pallava Bagla), 25 (Sukree Sukplang/ Reuters),
    27 (Bettmann), 34 (Mast Irham/ epa), 37 (Reuters).

Panos Pictures: cover/ title page (Tim A. Hetherington).

Science Photo Library: 5 (Gary Hincks), 6 (Sally Bensusen), 14 (Lynette Cook), 21 (Yalciner/ Kuran/ Taymaz),
    29 (George Bernard), 30 (Science Photo Library), 32, 33 (David A. Hardy), 38 (Alan Sirulnikoff), 39 (Digital Globe/
    Eurimage), 40 (Planetary Visions Ltd).

Shutterstock: 4 (A.S. Zain), 10 (Jarvis Gray), 23 (Norliza binti Azman).

TABLE OF CONTENTS

Glossary There is a glossary of terms on pages 45-46. Terms defined in the glossary are in type **that looks like this** on their first appearance on any spread (two facing pages).

Additional resources Books for further reading and recommended Web sites are listed on page 47. Because of the nature of the Internet, some Web site addresses may have changed since publication. The publisher has no responsibility for any such changes or for the content of cited sources.

WHAT IS A TSUNAMI?

A tsunami *(tsoo NAH mee)* is a series of powerful ocean waves caused by a sudden movement of seawater. A tsunami may result from an **earthquake,** a **landslide,** a volcanic **eruption,** or even an **asteroid** hitting Earth. When a big tsunami wave crashes onto shore it can be devastating. The water may smash boats and buildings, sweep away people and animals, and flood the land.

The start of a tsunami

A tsunami is caused by a large amount of water in the ocean being suddenly disturbed. For example, an undersea earthquake might push up a large piece of the **seabed,** moving the water above it. Or a mass of rock and soil from a landslide might fall into the sea, displacing a large amount of water. This sudden movement of water causes waves to spread out in all directions.

Houses in Aceh, Indonesia, were destroyed by the tsunami of 2004. The province of Aceh was especially hard hit; entire villages were swept away by the waves.

Giant waves

Out in the ocean, tsunami waves aren't very high. Tsunami waves in the deep ocean usually raise and lower the water level by 3 feet (1 meter) or less. A boat could sail over one of these waves without the boat's crew feeling it. These low tsunami waves, however, move very fast, traveling at up to 600 miles (970 kilometers) per hour. As a tsunami wave approaches the shallower water near land, the wave slows down to about 20 to 30 miles (30 to 50 kilometers) per hour. As the wave slows, all of the water that had been traveling so fast "piles up." This causes the wave to get higher and higher. By the time it hits the shore, a tsunami wave can be 100 feet (30 meters) in height—as high as a 10-story building.

1. A disturbance moves a large amount of water.

2. A low, fast wave moves outward from the disturbance.

3. As the wave nears land, it slows down.

4. The water slows and piles up, making the wave gain in height as it breaks onto the shore.

A tsunami wave.

Where do tsunamis happen?

Tsunamis occur most frequently in the Pacific Ocean, because this region has many earthquakes and volcanic eruptions. Tsunamis in the Pacific Ocean affect the coastlines of many countries, including Chile, Papua New Guinea *(PAH poo ah noo GIHN ee),* the Philippines, and Japan. In fact, the word *tsunami* comes from two Japanese words meaning "harbor" and "wave." Tsunamis can also occur in the Indian Ocean and the Atlantic Ocean. In fact, they can happen in any large body of water.

TSUNAMIS AND TIDAL WAVES

In the past, tsunamis were sometimes known as **tidal waves.** The term tidal wave is misleading, however, because tsunamis have nothing to do with **tides.** Tides are movements of water caused by variations in the gravitational pull of the moon and sun on different parts of Earth. Tides are regular events that can be predicted long before they occur. In fact, tide tables— charts giving the times and levels of the tides in a given area—are compiled and published a year in advance of the time they cover. Compare this with tsunamis, which happen only if something suddenly disturbs the water. A tsunami cannot be predicted until after the disturbance that triggers it has occurred.

WHAT CAUSES TSUNAMIS?

Tsunamis happen as a result of large-scale natural events, such as **earthquakes, landslides,** and volcanic **eruptions.** These events can cause huge movements of earth, rock, or ash. If these events occur on a **seabed,** on an island, or near a coast, the movement of these materials also disturbs the ocean water.

Earthquakes

Tsunamis are usually caused by earthquakes. The movement of Earth's **tectonic** *(tehk TON ihk)* **plates** causes most earthquakes. The movement of the plates strains the rock at and near plate boundaries and produces zones of **faults** around these boundaries. Along segments of some faults, the rock becomes locked in place and cannot slide as the plates move. Stress builds up in the rock on both sides of the fault. Finally, the rock breaks free and the ground moves suddenly. An earthquake like this caused the hugely destructive Indian Ocean tsunami of December 2004 (see page 18).

An earthquake on the seabed can cause a tsunami.

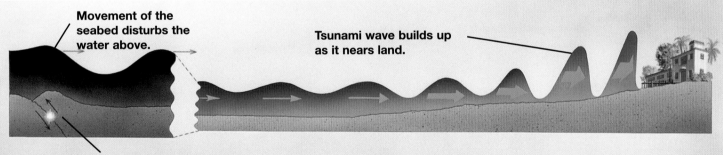

Movement of the seabed disturbs the water above.

Tsunami wave builds up as it nears land.

Earthquake causes the seabed to shift upward.

Volcanoes

Many **volcanoes** erupt quite slowly, throwing out **lava** and small lumps of rock. But if a lot of pressure builds up inside a volcano, it can erupt suddenly and blow away large portions of the volcano's cone. If the volcano lies underwater, near a coast, or on a small island, millions of tons of rock and ash can suddenly enter the sea.

The impact of the rock and ash can set off a tsunami. A large tsunami of this type was triggered by the eruption of Krakatau *(krah kuh TOW)*—sometimes called Krakatoa *(krah kuh TOH uh)*—a volcano in the Sunda Strait between the Indonesian islands of Sumatra *(soo MAH truh)* and Java *(JAH vuh)*. In 1883, the volcano Krakatau exploded in an enormous eruption heard nearly 3,000 miles (4,800 kilometers) away. The tsunami created by this eruption sent waves up to 130 feet (40 meters) high crashing to the shore (see page 12).

Landslides

A landslide is a mass of earth or rock that slides down a slope. Ground movements set off by earthquakes or volcanic eruptions sometimes cause landslides. Landslides can also occur when rain soaks into the soil on a slope, making the soil heavy and unstable. If a big landslide falls into the sea, it can displace a huge amount of water, creating a tsunami. In 1958, a massive landslide set off by an earthquake created the highest tsunami wave on record, at Lituya *(lih TOO yuh)* Bay, Alaska (see page 26).

TSUNAMIS FROM SPACE

An **asteroid** is a large chunk of rock or metal that **orbits** the sun. Millions of asteroids may exist. Occasionally, an asteroid comes close to Earth and is pulled in by Earth's **gravity.** Most of these asteroids break up in Earth's atmosphere before reaching the planet's surface. If such an asteroid were ever to land in an ocean, however, it could cause a huge tsunami (see page 32). There is no conclusive proof that this has happened, but a group of scientists are now studying the southwestern coast of Madagascar. These scientists believe that the **geology** of Madagascar's coast and a large **crater** found in the seabed of the Indian Ocean are evidence of an asteroid striking the Indian Ocean about 4,800 years ago. The tsunami wave that resulted is theorized to have been approximately 600 feet (180 meters) high.

An earthquake caused this landslide on a coastal cliff in California.

THE CHILEAN TSUNAMI

One of the biggest **earthquakes** ever recorded took place on May 22, 1960. It shook the floor of the Pacific Ocean, 100 miles (160 kilometers) off the coast of Chile. The movement of the **seabed** created a tsunami that raced out across the Pacific.

Chile

Just 15 minutes after the earthquake, the tsunami struck the coast of Chile. As the initial wave reached the shore, it rose up to a towering wall of water, in some places up to 80 feet (25 meters) high. A series of waves devastated over 500 miles (800 kilometers) of coastline, from the city of Concepción (kuhn sehp see OHN) in the north to the island of Chiloé (chee loh AY) in the south. On Chiloé, many people had set sail near the shore in small boats to avoid the shaking of the earthquake. The boats were swamped by the tsunami and more than 200 islanders drowned. In all, about 2,000 people died in Chile, as the waves flattened seashore villages and flooded the coast up to ⅓ mile (0.5 kilometer) inland.

The spread of the Chilean tsunami across the Pacific Ocean in May 1960.

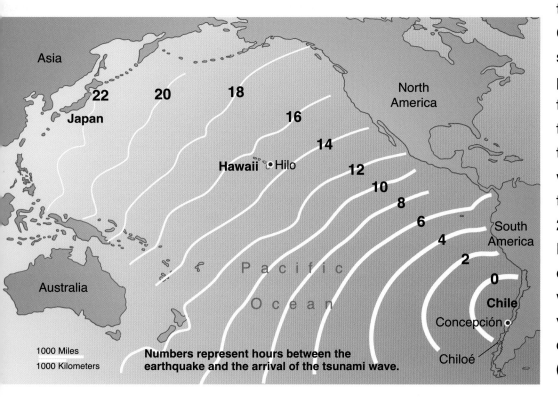

Asia

22 20 18

Japan

16

14

Hawaii Hilo

12

10

8

6

4

2

0

North America

South America

Chile

Concepción

Chiloé

Pacific

Ocean

Australia

1000 Miles
1000 Kilometers

Numbers represent hours between the earthquake and the arrival of the tsunami wave.

Across the ocean

As the waves subsided in Chile, the tsunami was still spreading out across the Pacific Ocean. It headed toward Hawaii, an island chain in the middle of the ocean. Fifteen hours after the earthquake, a series of tsunami waves struck the town of Hilo (HEE loh), on

Hawaii's biggest island. The tallest waves reached over 30 feet (10 meters) high. Hundreds of buildings and cars were destroyed, and 61 people were killed. Finally, 22 hours after the earthquake, the tsunami struck Japan, 10,000 miles (16,000 kilometers) from where the earthquake took place, and killed another 138 people.

People in Hilo, Hawaii, look out on houses and roads wrecked by the Chilean tsunami.

Near and far

If a tsunami's destructive effects only reach the coast near the point of its origin, it is a **local tsunami.** One that travels thousands of miles across the ocean is called a **transoceanic** *(TRANS oh shee AN ihk)* **tsunami,** or a teletsunami *(TEHL uh tsoo NAH mee).* Transoceanic tsunamis are less common than local tsunamis, but transoceanics are often the most deadly. The Chilean tsunami of 1960 and the tsunami of 2004 (see page 18) were both transoceanic in nature.

WAVE AFTER WAVE

Before the Chilean tsunami struck Hilo in Hawaii, the authorities knew it was on the way. They sounded sirens to warn people to move away from the coast. But after the first wave struck, many people went back to the shore, thinking it was safe. They were caught in later, even bigger waves. A tsunami is usually made up of a series of waves—and the first is not always the biggest or the most dangerous.

WHAT MAKES UP A TSUNAMI?

A tsunami is made up of a series of waves. Waves carry energy and are disturbances in water, air, or other substances. As a wave passes through water, its energy makes the water level rise. The water falls again after the wave passes by. Unlike tides, which are mostly caused by gravitational forces, normal ocean waves are mostly caused by the wind. But with these normal waves, it is only the surface of the ocean that is affected. Tsunami waves affect an entire column of water in the ocean from the seabed to the surface. Far more energy is involved in moving that much water, but the types of events, such as earthquakes, that trigger a tsunami release a lot of energy.

Normal ocean waves are mostly caused by the wind.

Parts of a wave

A wave has several different parts. The highest point of a wave is called the **crest.** The lowest part is the **trough** *(trawf).* The distance from the crest of one wave to the crest of the next wave is called the **wavelength.** The material that a wave travels through—such as water—is called the **wave medium.** The height of a wave above the normal level of the wave medium is called the **amplitude.**

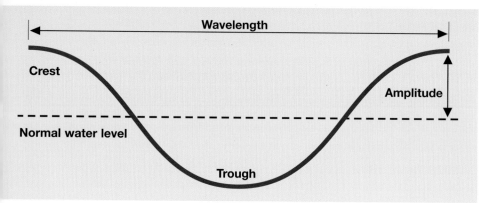

The different parts of a wave.

Tsunami waves

When tsunami waves travel across an ocean, they have a long wavelength, measuring up to 300 miles (500 kilometers). Ordinary waves created by wind have a much shorter wavelength, that ranges from around 2 feet (0.6 meter) to 1,000 feet (300 meters). Tsunami waves also have a low amplitude, often about 3 feet (1 meter).

Tsunami waves move fast across the ocean— the deeper the water, the faster they travel. While waves generated by wind may move anywhere from around 2 to 60 miles (3.2 to 97 kilometers) per hour, tsunami waves can travel at speeds of 600 miles (970 kilometers) per hour, the speed of a jet airplane.

As a tsunami wave moves into shallow water, it gets slower and its wavelength gets shorter. This happens because the front of the wave "drags" on the **seabed** and slows down. But the rest of the wave is still moving fast, and it "catches up" with the front. The water that was previously in a long, flat wave piles up into a shorter, very high wave.

As the wave approaches the land, the water along the shoreline can be pulled out to sea, receding far beyond the normal low-**tide** mark. The water then rushes in again as the crest of the wave follows, flooding the coast with a huge surge of water.

BREAKING WAVES

As an ordinary ocean wave nears the shore, it drags on the seafloor and begins to tip forward. Most tsunami waves do not crest like a usual wave, which curls over at the top as it approaches the shore. Instead, some tsunami waves look like an almost vertical wall of churning water coming in. Others look more like an advancing tide of very fast-rising water. Either way, water rushes over the land, flooding low-lying areas. The farthest distance inland (horizontally) reached by the tsunami waters is referred to as the area of **inundation.** The highest point (vertically) that this water reaches is called the **run up.** Even if the tsunami comes in as a large wall of water, the height of the run up may be higher than the height of the wave.

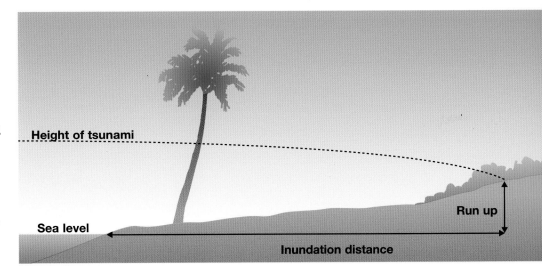

How inundation and run up are measured, as the water from a tsunami flows onto the land.

KILLER KRAKATAU

Krakatau is an island and **volcano** between the Indonesian islands of Java and Sumatra. Krakatau has erupted many times, but the most famous **eruption** took place in August 1883. This was also Krakatau's deadliest eruption, because of the tsunami it created.

The eruption

In May 1883, the volcano Krakatau awoke after more than 200 years of inactivity. Over the next few months, passing ships and local villagers on nearby islands saw and heard a series of small eruptions as the volcano blew out

Ash and steam pour out of the volcano Krakatau in an illustration from 1883.

Krakatau lies between Java and Sumatra, in Indonesia.

Philippines

Malaysia

INDONESIA

Sumatra

Lampong Bay

Sebuku

Sebesi

Java Sea

Sunda Strait

Krakatau

Java

Indian Ocean

East Timor

Australia

500 Miles

500 Kilometers

jets of steam and clouds of volcanic gas. The eruptions became stronger until, on August 27, a series of four massive, explosive blasts blew apart the cone of the volcano. The last and biggest eruption made the loudest sound known in history. It was heard almost 3,000 miles (4,800 kilometers) away on the island of Rodrigues *(roh DREE gehs)* in the Indian Ocean.

Shock-wave tsunamis

The first three explosions of Krakatau on August 27 are thought to have created small, tsunami-like waves caused by atmospheric shock. This means that blasts of air from the explosions, called concussions, caused waves of air that pushed down on the sea surface, creating a ripple effect. These waves, however, were not deadly. There was worse to come when the cone of Krakatau exploded and rained down into the sea.

The big one

The fourth explosive eruption blew Krakatau to pieces, releasing over 6 cubic miles (25 cubic kilometers) of rock and ash. To get some idea of how much material that is, you could fill New York City's 102-story Empire State Building more than 20,000 times with the **ejecta** *(ih JEHK tuh)* spewed from Krakatau in this eruption. Much of this ejecta plunged into the sea. At the same time, a huge **crater** formed where a large part of the volcano had once been, and seawater was sucked into it. All of these disturbances in the ocean created enormous tsunami waves that reached heights of up to 130 feet (40 meters).

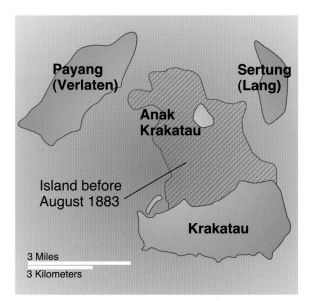

Much of the volcano of Krakatau is underwater, but some of it projects above, forming the islands of Krakatau, Anak Krakatau, Payang (Verlaten), and Sertung (Lang).

SAILING OVER A TSUNAMI

As the tsunami waves raced toward the surrounding islands, ships at sea were the first to encounter them. A passenger steamship, the *Loudon*, was in Lampong Bay on the south coast of Sumatra as the tsunami approached. One of the passengers later recalled: "Suddenly we saw a gigantic wave of prodigious height advancing toward the seashore with considerable speed. ... The ship met the wave head on and the *Loudon* was lifted up with a dizzying rapidity and made a formidable leap. ... The ship rode at a high angle over the crest of the wave and down the other side."

Washed away

The island of Krakatau is surrounded by other islands. The tsunami waves caused by the **eruption** on Krakatau in 1883 did not travel far before reaching the shorelines of Sumatra, Java, and other nearby islands. There, these waves caused enormous destruction and devastation.

Only 8 miles (13 kilometers) to the north of Krakatau lies the island of Sebesi *(suh BUH see)*. The island of Krakatau was uninhabited, but more than 3,000 people lived on Sebesi in 1883. The island had already been showered with burning-hot ash and rock from the eruption. When the tsunami waves arrived, water swept right over the island, washing all the inhabitants out to sea. None are known to have survived.

Tsunami tragedy

About an hour after the explosion, tsunami waves began to strike the shores of the larger islands of Java and Sumatra. There was little warning. People in coastal villages and even those working far inland in the rice fields suddenly heard a roaring noise. They saw a

An artist's interpretation of a giant tsunami wave caused by the 1883 eruption of Krakatau.

churning wall of water rushing toward them. People tried to climb trees or run to higher ground, but for most it was too late. Hundreds of villages were destroyed and boats smashed. Thousands of people were washed away. In all, the Dutch authorities (who controlled Indonesia at the time) estimated that more than 36,000 lives were lost.

Worldwide effects

The tsunami waves spread out across the Indian Ocean, but they did not cause disaster on distant shores because the islands around Krakatau acted as a barrier. By the time the waves reached India and Africa, they were little bigger than normal ocean waves.

Child of Krakatau

In 1927, volcanic activity began again at the site of Krakatau, and a new volcanic island emerged from the sea. It is known as Anak Krakatau, meaning "child of Krakatau." The region remains volcanically active. One day, another huge eruption creating more tsunamis is likely to take place here.

Anak Krakatau rises out of the lagoon left behind by the explosion of the volcano Krakatau. A plume of ejecta from Anak Krakatau is visible here.

DUST AT SUNSET

When Krakatau exploded, it blasted dust and ash high into Earth's **atmosphere**. The dust and ash floated around the planet for many months, causing vivid, bright-red sunsets. The dust also blocked out the sun's heat, leading to an unusually cold winter and summer.

Piles of debris fill the streets of Banda Aceh, Indonesia, after the tsunami of December 2004.

DESTROYING LIVES

Many of the deadliest natural disasters in history have involved tsunamis. Tsunamis are especially devastating when they hit a heavily populated area. In many countries, large numbers of people live along coastlines, either in cities or in smaller settlements, where they make a living from tourism and fishing. So the very places where tsunamis strike are often places where many people visit or live.

Swept away

The first thing that happens when a tsunami wave strikes is that people are swept off their feet and carried away by the fast-flowing water. After a tsunami wave surges onto the shore, the water eventually retreats, pulling people out to sea. In such strong **currents,** it's hard to swim or stay afloat. A person who is swept away is likely to drown.

Smashing and crushing

A tsunami wave doesn't just pick up people and small objects. The force of the wave can smash entire buildings and wash away bridges and traffic lights. It can lift up cars and boats and carry them for miles before dropping them back down. When a tsunami wave hits a town or village, everything may be broken to pieces. People may get crushed inside collapsing buildings and battered by rubble and **debris.**

The aftermath

Even after the waves of a tsunami have passed, danger remains. Weakened buildings and piles of debris can collapse unexpectedly. If power and water supplies are cut off and roads are blocked, survivors can suffer from a lack of food and safe shelter and from diseases spread by dirty drinking water and leaking **sewage.**

WATER POWER

Water is very heavy—a gallon of water weighs 8.34 pounds (3.78 kilograms)—so when a large amount of it is moving fast, it has enormous force. Even shallow, knee-deep water can easily sweep a person away if it is flowing fast. So a tsunami wave 30 feet (9 meters) high can sweep away everything in its path.

Indian tsunami survivors repairing a roof in Nagapattinam, southern India, after the 2004 tsunami.

THE TSUNAMI OF 2004

On December 26, 2004, at around 7:58 a.m., a huge **earthquake** shook the **seabed** off the coast of Sumatra in Indonesia. The quake triggered one of the biggest, most destructive tsunamis ever known.

Indian Ocean tsunami

Tsunamis are most common in the Pacific Ocean, but the huge tsunami of 2004 affected the Indian Ocean, where there was no warning system (see page 34). The tsunami took many of its victims by surprise. As the waves spread outward over the course of seven hours, they first hit Sumatra. After that, the Andaman and Nicobar Islands (a territory of India in the Bay of Bengal) were hit. The waves then reached the coast of Thailand and parts of the western coasts of Myanmar and Malaysia. Later, Sri Lanka and the coast of the Indian mainland were struck by tsunami waves. Finally, the waves reached the islands of Maldives *(MAWL deevz)* and the coast of East Africa on the far side of the Indian Ocean, striking mainly Somalia but also parts of Kenya and Tanzania.

The epicenter of the earthquake that caused the tsunami of 2004 and the areas worst affected by it.

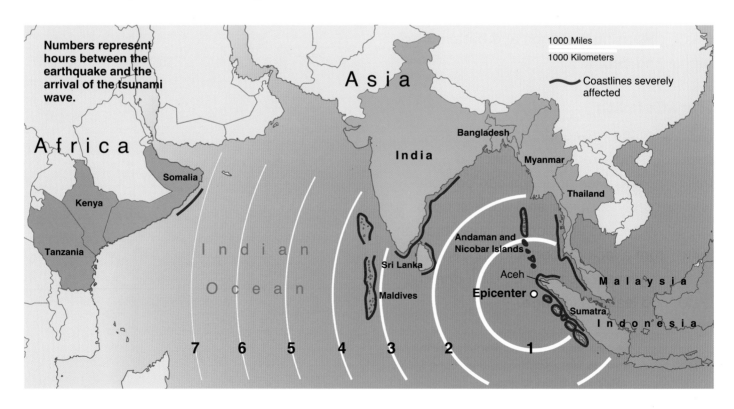

Terrible toll

The tsunami is thought to have killed more than 216,000 people—possibly as many as 283,000. It claimed so many lives partly because it was so large and widespread. It was also deadly because it hit densely populated shorelines filled with towns and cities, fishing harbors, and busy tourist resorts. Victims included not only local people but also tourists from such countries as Australia, Sweden, the United Kingdom, and the United States, who were spending their Christmas vacations at beach resorts in Southeast Asia.

Surviving the tsunami

The people who saw the tsunami coming ran for their lives, though there was little time to escape. Some people managed to climb trees and cling to the branches as the water swept past. Others ran to the highest ground they could find or survived on the upper floors of buildings that withstood the waves. On one beach in Phuket *(poo KEHT),* Thailand, a 10-year-old British tourist, Tilly Smith, recognized the signs of a tsunami when the sea retreated, leaving the seabed bare (see page 11). She warned everyone to run away from the shore, saving many lives.

EYEWITNESS ACCOUNTS

Swedish survivor Boree Carlsson describes how the tsunami hit a beach in Thailand: "We heard screaming as a great surge came over the beach and onto the road, flooding the shops and hotel garden. The beach umbrellas and sunbeds were like dolls' furniture as they were swept inland. The surge continued, and dozens of cars were swept along the road like floating toys."

Daya Wijaya Gunawardana from Sri Lanka describes being in a train flooded by the tsunami: "The train had stopped at signals. Then suddenly sea flooded through the train, very high, very quick... the whole train was filled with water. Then it fell over. I thought that we were killed, that we were dead... but I got up to a window and escaped."

The third, and largest, wave of the 2004 tsunami crashing over Ao Nang Beach in Thailand.

Shifting plates

The **earthquake** that caused the 2004 tsunami was one of the strongest on record. Some researchers calculated a 9.3 **moment magnitude** for the quake. Not all scientists have verified and accepted these calculations, but all agree that the earthquake was so violent it made the whole planet wobble.

The earthquake happened at the boundary between two **tectonic plates.** Near Indonesia, the Indian-Australian Plate pushes down beneath another plate, called the Burma Plate, which is often considered a piece of the larger Eurasian Plate. Scientists think that the Indian-Australian Plate had begun to pull the Burma Plate down with it, putting Earth's **crust** under huge stress. Finally, on December 26, 2004, the Burma plate suddenly sprang back into place, causing a huge section of the **seabed** to shift upward. The movement of the seabed pushed the ocean up as well, triggering the tsunami.

Above, January 2003; below, December 2004

Satellite images showing the town of Lhoknga, in Indonesia, before and after the tsunami of 2004.

Side to side

During the earthquake that caused the tsunami, a long section of seabed moved. This means that the tsunami did not start from a single point but, instead, began along a long line stretching from north to south. As a result, the waves moving west and east from the earthquake were more powerful than those moving north and south. Because of that, countries to the west and east of the earthquake's **epicenter,** such as Sri Lanka and Thailand, sustained more damage than those to the north or south, such as Bangladesh and Australia.

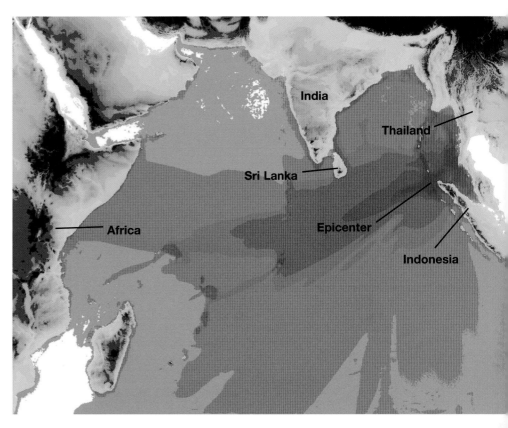

A computer-generated map showing changes in the height of the sea surface as a tsunami wave passed through the Indian Ocean in 2004. The darkest red areas show where the wave was highest.

Tsunami on the way

The tsunami waves traveled across the ocean at speeds of up to 500 miles (800 kilometers) per hour. **Satellite** measurements revealed that out at sea the waves were only about 2 feet (0.6 meter) high. But as the waves approached the coastline of Indonesia and slowed down, they reached heights of up to 100 feet (30 meters). As they passed islands and **headlands,** the waves "wrapped" themselves around the land and changed direction—an effect known as **refraction.** This resulted in greater devastation across a larger area.

TSUNAMI TRAVEL TIMES

This chart shows how long it took the tsunami to reach the main countries it affected after being triggered in the southeast Indian Ocean near Indonesia.

Sumatra, Indonesia	15 minutes
Andaman and Nicobar Islands	30 minutes
Thailand, Myanmar, Malaysia	90 minutes
Sri Lanka, Indian mainland	2 hours
Maldives	3.5 hours
Somalia, Kenya, Tanzania	7 hours

Sending help

As news of the tsunami disaster spread around the globe, many countries, charities, and individuals joined to help with rescue efforts. The tsunami had caused a huge amount of destruction. The United Nations estimated that cleaning up and rebuilding all the damaged areas would take at least four years.

First on the scene

The first tasks facing rescuers and aid workers included searching for survivors, recovering bodies, and caring for the sick and injured. Governments and charity organizations sent military staff, emergency services, doctors, and aid workers to help.

Many people were rescued from beneath collapsed buildings. Others were found alive after being swept across the land by the waves. A few survivors were even found at sea, days after the tsunami, clinging to floating branches. Meanwhile, the bodies of those who had died had to be identified, then buried or cremated. Medical charities set up field hospitals to treat injuries. Photos were put up on bulletin boards and Internet message boards to try to help separated families and friends find each other.

Indian soldiers remove a damaged fishing boat from a beach in southern India, as part of the clean-up effort after the 2004 tsunami.

Starting again

While many thousands died, millions of others were left without shelter, clothing, food, or clean water. In some towns, people moved into any buildings that remained standing—usually the biggest, strongest buildings, such as mosques, temples, and government headquarters. Governments and aid agencies tried to ensure that even in the most remote areas, essential supplies reached survivors. Since 2004, those who survived the tsunami have faced the huge task of clearing away the **debris** and mud and rebuilding residences and businesses. In some places, it will take years to recover farmland that has been ruined by salt water. Other places, however, have quickly rebuilt and redeveloped their tourist industries. Meanwhile, scientists and governments have worked together to set up a tsunami warning system for the Indian Ocean to try to prevent such a tragedy from happening again.

Many tsunami survivors in Aceh, Indonesia, lived in this refugee camp until their homes could be rebuilt.

TSUNAMIS AND THE ENVIRONMENT

When a tsunami wave comes ashore, it can affect a huge area of land, transforming the landscape. Tsunamis can also have long-term effects on the sea by releasing pollution into the water. As a result, the environment can take many years to recover from a tsunami's deluge.

Ruining the land

A tsunami wave throws salty seawater over the land. Too much salt is bad for living things, so if soil becomes too salty, crops cannot grow or will not grow well. The force of tsunami waves can also wreck pipelines and factories, releasing **sewage,** oil, or dangerous chemicals into the environment. It can take many years for the pollution to disperse and for the environment to return to normal.

Natural protection

Along some coastlines, **coral reefs** or mangrove forests provide natural protection against tsunamis. A coral reef is mostly a framework of skeletons from marine animals called corals. A reef near the shore can absorb much of a tsunami's impact before it reaches land. Mangroves are trees that grow along tropical coasts in salty ocean water.

A coral reef in the Nicobar island group that was badly damaged by the 2004 tsunami.

Some types of mangrove form a network of many stiltlike roots that supports the tree's leafy crown above the water. Mangroves can also act as a buffer when a tsunami strikes, absorbing the wave's energy before it surges onto the shore.

Plants and animals

Like humans, animals can be washed away and drowned by a tsunami wave. This is especially true of livestock that are kept in pens. Sea creatures also suffer when a tsunami strikes. Fish, whales, dolphins, and turtles can be swept onto the land by the waves; often, they are stranded as the water retreats. The water of a tsunami flows so fast that it can strip land of crops and other plants and even uproot trees. Certain plants, however, are adapted to survive high winds and large waves. Palm trees, for example, with their long, bare trunks, are well adapted to life on the shore and often survive tsunamis intact.

CAN ANIMALS SENSE TSUNAMIS?

After the tsunami of 2004, people noticed that very few wild animals were harmed by the waves. It seems that animals such as elephants moved to higher ground before the tsunami hit. Scientists think that some animals can detect when a tsunami is on its way. Perhaps people may eventually be able to make use of this animal ability to help with warning systems for tsunamis.

During the 2004 tsunami, 20 turtles died at a hatchery in Phuket, Thailand, where endangered turtles are bred to be released into the wild. Here, scientists are carefully carrying one of the 80 surviving turtles to safety.

THE LITUYA BAY MEGATSUNAMI

The term **megatsunami** *(MEHG uh tsoo NAH mee)* is sometimes used to describe a tsunami with extremely high waves. A normal tsunami wave might reach about 30 feet (9 meters) high, and many are much smaller. A megatsunami can be more than 1,000 feet (300 meters) high. These enormous tsunami waves are usually caused by large amounts of water being displaced in a confined area, such as a small bay. The megatsunami at Lituya Bay, Alaska, in 1958, was the tallest tsunami wave ever recorded.

Lituya landslide

Lituya Bay, in Alaska, is surrounded by mountains that almost completely enclose the bay. In July 1958, an **earthquake** shook the mountains, causing a vast **landslide.** A mass of rock and soil slipped down a steep hillside into the deep waters of the bay, forcing up a huge wave. No one knows exactly how high the wave was, but as it washed over a **headland** in the bay, it stripped the land bare of trees up to a height of 1,720 feet (516 meters).

This headland in Lituya Bay, Alaska, remains largely treeless fully 14 years after the 1958 tsunami stripped it of nearly all vegetation.

As the first giant wave subsided, a smaller—but still enormous—wave, traveled the length of the bay.

The area was mostly uninhabited, but two people died when their small boats were washed out to sea. Another boat, carrying fisherman Howard Ulrich and his seven-year-old son, safely sailed right over the wave, and both father and son survived.

More megatsunamis

Megatsunamis are usually caused by landslides. In 1980, when Mount Saint Helens erupted in Washington State, it sent a huge landslide into nearby Spirit Lake, creating a megatsunami wave 800 feet (240 meters) high. Another inland tsunami occurred at the Vajont Dam in Italy in 1963, when a landslide fell into the reservoir behind the dam. A giant wave, 820 feet (250 meters) high, surged over the top of the dam and flooded several villages in the valley below. More than 2,000 people were killed.

The ruined remains of a village in Italy destroyed by the Vajont Dam tsunami in 1963.

TSUNAMIS IN THE ATLANTIC

Tsunamis are relatively rare in the Atlantic Ocean. This is mainly because **earthquakes** and **volcanoes** are less common in the Atlantic than in the Pacific and Indian oceans. However, there have been some very large and famous Atlantic tsunamis.

The Grand Banks tsunami

In 1929, an immense earthquake rocked the Grand Banks, an area of shallow sea off the coast of Newfoundland, Canada. The earthquake caused an undersea **landslide,** triggering three huge tsunami waves. When they crashed onto the shores of Newfoundland and Nova Scotia, the waves reached heights of up to 23 feet (7 meters), killing 29 people.

Caribbean tsunamis

The Caribbean Sea, on the west side of the Atlantic Ocean, is a high-risk area for tsunamis. It has deep undersea trenches and volcanoes that can trigger earthquakes and landslides on the **seabed.** It also has many small islands, where tsunami waves can

Although rare in the Atlantic, tsunamis hit Lisbon in 1755; the Virgin Islands in 1867; Newfoundland in 1929; and the Dominican Republic in 1946. Scientists fear that an eruption of the Cumbre Vieja volcano off the Canary Islands could trigger a megatsunami that might affect major coastal cities, including Boston, Miami, and New York.

cause havoc as they wash ashore. In 1867, a tsunami hit the Virgin Islands after an undersea earthquake. It carried dozens of boats, including large steamships, onto the shore. Another earthquake off the Dominican Republic in 1946 caused a tsunami that killed 1,800 people.

The next megatsunami?

In the Canary Islands, off the coast of northwest Africa, the Cumbre Vieja volcano is poised to cause a **megatsunami**. Scientists predict that when it next erupts, half of the volcano could collapse in a vast landslide. This could deposit up to 120 cubic miles (500 cubic kilometers) of rock into the sea. Some scientists believe that the resulting tsunami could cross the Atlantic Ocean and devastate U.S. coastal cities, such as New York, Boston, and Miami, with waves more than 100 feet (30 meters) high.

A period illustration depicts the steamship *La Plata* caught in the Virgin Islands tsunami of 1867.

WAITING FOR THE WAVE

When the tsunami struck the Virgin Islands in 1867, Admiral James S. Palmer of the U.S. Navy went up to the deck of his ship, the U.S.S. *Susquehanna,* to see the wave approaching the harbor. He wrote: "The report was brought to me that the sea outside of the harbour had risen and was coming in a huge volume as if to engulf us all. ... With a feeling of awe we awaited its arrival; it came rushing on, tumbling over the rocks that formed the entrance, carrying everything before it." In December of the same year, Palmer died in the Virgin Islands of yellow fever.

THE LISBON TSUNAMI

An enormous **earthquake** caused the Lisbon tsunami of 1755. The **epicenter** of the earthquake was on the Atlantic **seabed,** about 125 miles (200 kilometers) off the coast of Portugal. The earthquake and tsunami together are thought to have killed as many as 100,000 people.

Earthquake horror

The earthquake was felt across western Europe. The shaking of the ground made church bells ring in Paris, and tremors reached as far as Finland. In Portugal's capital, Lisbon, the earthquake caused buildings to collapse and opened up huge cracks in the ground. Many of the city's terrified citizens rushed to the shore for safety. There, they were amazed to see the seawater rushing away from the shore, revealing the seabed scattered with sea creatures and sunken boats. This was a sign that a tsunami wave was about to hit.

A period illustration depicts the destruction of Lisbon caused by the tsunami of 1755 and the resulting fires that broke out among the ruins.

Surging into the streets

Minutes later, the tsunami arrived. Eyewitnesses said the wave measured between 20 feet (6 meters) and 50 feet (15 meters) high as it roared into the city. It surged at least half a mile (0.8 kilometer) onto the land and rushed up the city's streets. It smashed into buildings, wrecked boats on the river, and swept people and animals out to sea. The first wave was followed by two more. Most of the city of Lisbon was flattened, and about 90,000 of its residents were killed.

Around the Atlantic

The tsunami spread out in all directions across the Atlantic Ocean. Huge waves hit Tangier, Morocco; Cadiz, Spain; and the Canary and Azores islands. The tsunami claimed thousands more lives around southwest Europe and North Africa. Smaller waves came ashore in Wales and Ireland, ripping boats from their moorings. Tsunami waves also traveled 3,500 miles (5,600 kilometers) across the Atlantic Ocean to the Caribbean islands of Antigua and Barbados.

The Lisbon tsunami spread out in all directions from the earthquake that shook the seabed near Portugal.

A WRITER'S RESPONSE

The Lisbon disaster shocked Europe, and many writers and philosophers discussed what it could mean. The French writer and philosopher Voltaire (1694-1778) included a description of the disaster in his novel *Candide*: "They perceived that the earth trembled under their feet, and the sea, swelling and foaming in the harbor, was dashing in pieces the vessels that were riding at anchor. ... The houses tottered and were tumbled topsy-turvy even to their foundations."

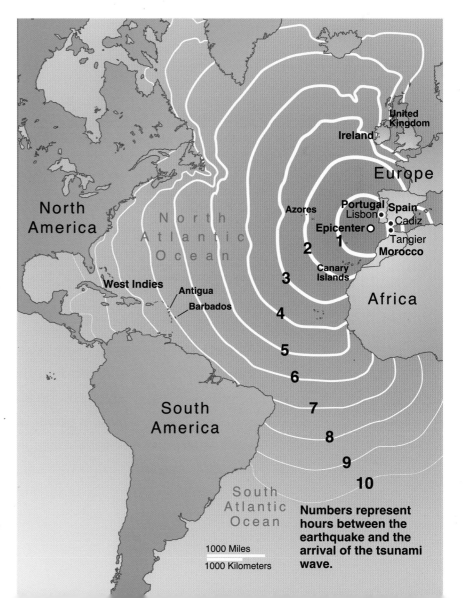

Numbers represent hours between the earthquake and the arrival of the tsunami wave.

1000 Miles
1000 Kilometers

An artist's impression showing an asteroid approaching Earth.

TSUNAMIS AND ASTEROIDS

Seas and oceans cover about 70 percent of Earth's surface, which means if an **asteroid** collided with Earth, it would probably land in water. Such an asteroid impact could trigger a tsunami or even a **megatsunami,** which could cause disaster.

What is an asteroid?

An **asteroid** is a small body made of rock, carbon, or metal that travels through space **orbiting** the sun. There may be millions of asteroids. They range from the size of a pebble up to the largest asteroid, Ceres, which is about 580 miles (930 kilometers) across. Most asteroids, however, measure less than 6 miles (10 kilometers) across. Sometimes, when an asteroid's orbit brings it close to Earth, the Earth's **gravity** pulls the asteroid in. Earth's atmosphere protects the planet from most asteroid strikes. Air **friction** will disintegrate an asteroid smaller than about 160 feet (50 meters) in diameter before it can reach the surface. But in some instances, larger asteroids have landed on Earth's surface.

An asteroid tsunami

An asteroid falling to Earth would be moving at up to 60,000 miles (100,000 kilometers) per hour. If such an asteroid landed in the sea, a huge volume of water would be instantly **vaporized,** leaving a vast empty area in the sea— a "hole"—where that water once was. Water would rush in from all sides to fill the hole, creating a giant wave. Tsunami waves would then spread outward from this point.

The size of a tsunami caused by an asteroid would depend on the size and speed of the asteroid and where it landed. In shallow water, an asteroid could create tsunami waves from 400 feet (120 meters) to more than 1 mile (1.6 kilometers) high. Depending on where the asteroid landed, a megatsunami like that could wipe out hundreds of cities and kill millions of people.

TSUNAMIS AND THE DINOSAURS

About 65 million years ago, an asteroid fell to Earth that measured around 6 miles (10 kilometers) in diameter. It landed in the sea just off the Yucatán peninsula, in what is now Mexico. Unusual deposits of rock that washed from the **seabed** onto the shore show that the asteroid probably caused huge tsunamis, several miles high. The tsunamis could have been a factor that contributed to the **extinction** of the dinosaurs, which also happened about 65 million years ago.

An artist's impression of the asteroid that hit Earth 65 million years ago. That was too early to affect humans, but scientists think this asteroid was a major disaster for the dinosaurs.

TSUNAMI WARNING SYSTEMS

Tsunamis are so large and powerful that even the most advanced technology cannot stop them. But scientists have found ways to detect tsunamis and to predict when they will hit land. Tsunami warning systems can now forecast some tsunamis hours before they arrive, giving those at risk time to escape.

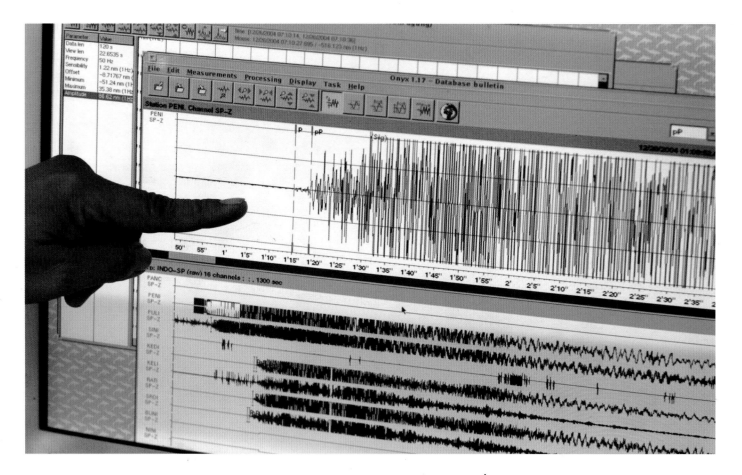

A recording of the ground motion captured by a seismograph during the earthquake that caused the 2004 tsunami.

Detecting the trigger

Most tsunamis are caused by **earthquakes** on the **seabed** or by volcanic **eruptions.** Scientists use machines called **seismographs** *(SYZ muh grafz)* to record **seismic** *(SYZ mihk)* **waves.** For example, scientists can pinpoint where an undersea earthquake has occurred and calculate the path of the tsunami triggered by the earthquake. However, not all earthquakes and eruptions cause tsunamis, so this system alone isn't enough.

To detect tsunamis more accurately, scientists need to measure the movements of seawater as well.

Detecting the wave

There are two main ways to detect a tsunami wave as it races across the ocean. One is to measure the depth of the water near the coast using a **tidal gauge.** This is a device with **sensors** that detect the water level. A tidal gauge can sense the rise in sea level as a tsunami passes by, but it cannot warn of a tsunami very far in advance of the event.

The *Deep-ocean Assessment and Reporting of Tsunamis* (DART) system detects tsunamis using pressure sensors on the seabed that measure the weight of water above them. As the crest of a tsunami wave passes, the sensors register the excess weight of the water moving overhead. As a trough passes, the weight of the water overhead drops, Thus, DART sensors can detect a tsunami wave far out at sea. When a sensor detects such a change, the information is relayed to a **satellite.** Scientists can use the information to predict when and where a tsunami will strike and can then send out warnings to the governments of the countries concerned.

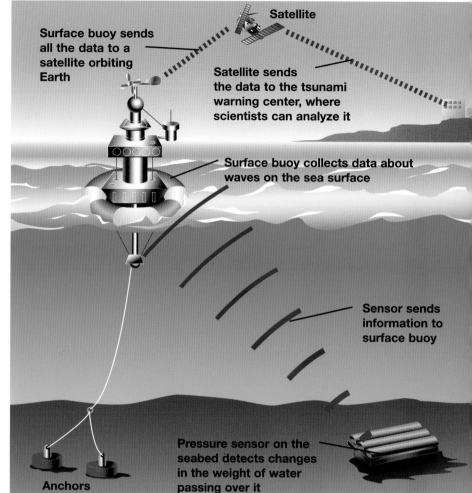

Surface buoy sends all the data to a satellite orbiting Earth

Satellite

Satellite sends the data to the tsunami warning center, where scientists can analyze it

Surface buoy collects data about waves on the sea surface

Sensor sends information to surface buoy

Pressure sensor on the seabed detects changes in the weight of water passing over it

Anchors

How the DART pressure-sensor system works.

THE ITWS

The first tsunami warning centers were set up to monitor and predict tsunamis in the Pacific Ocean. But since the devastating tsunami of 2004, governments have started to set up tidal gauges and DART sensors in the Indian Ocean, as well. There is now an *International Tsunami Warning System* (ITWS), based in Hawaii, in the Pacific Ocean. The system collects data from stations and sensors all around the world and releases warnings to about 30 countries that have a high likelihood of tsunamis.

WARNING SYSTEMS IN ACTION— THE TSUNAMI AT OKUSHIRI

An **earthquake** on the **seabed** off northern Japan caused a huge tsunami in 1993. Scientists detected the earthquake, and the Japanese authorities quickly acted to send out tsunami warnings. Although some people could not be warned in time, thousands of lives were saved.

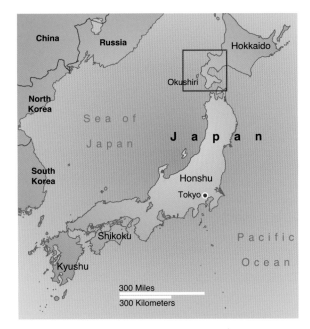

The Okushiri earthquake

The earthquake struck at 10:17 p.m. on July 12, 1993. Its **epicenter** was about 40 miles (64 kilometers) off the small island of Okushiri *(oh koo SHEE ree).* The earthquake was large; **seismographs** measured it at a 7.8 **moment magnitude.** Scientists issued a tsunami alert just five minutes after the earthquake occurred. They warned people on the coasts of Japan and other countries nearby to escape to safety.

Island disaster

On Okushiri itself, the warnings came too late because the tsunami wave took only three minutes to reach the island. A vast wave, up to 100 feet (30 meters) high according to some reports, swept over part of the island and swamped the town of Aonae. The people of Okushiri had experienced tsunamis before, and many had started to head for safety as soon as they felt the ground shake. Nevertheless, more than 200 islanders died.

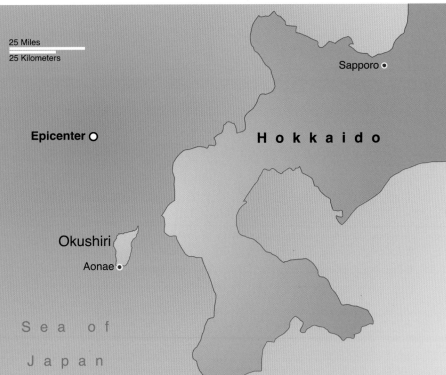

The Japanese island of Okushiri, just south of the epicenter, was hit by a vast wave only three minutes after the 7.8 magnitude earthquake.

Survivors standing among collapsed houses after a tsunami flattened the town of Aonae in 1993.

Evacuation

Farther away, on the larger Japanese island of Hokkaido *(hah KY doh),* there was more time to evacuate. Thousands of people who lived along the coast managed to escape. After the tsunami, reports revealed that those who had used their cars to drive away from the danger got stuck in traffic jams and were therefore more likely to be swept away by the wave. The reports showed that the best way to escape was on foot, climbing up any steep slopes nearby as quickly as possible.

A WARNING THAT DIDN'T WORK

A tsunami triggered by another big earthquake killed more than 600 people in Java, Indonesia, in July 2006. A tsunami warning was sent to the Indonesian government with 45 minutes to spare. But the government did not want to cause unnecessary alarm, and the message did not reach the coast in time. This experience showed that warnings have to be taken seriously and broadcast as fast as possible.

TSUNAMI PREPARATION AND SURVIVAL

When a tsunami strikes, escaping it and surviving are sometimes a matter of luck. But there are some ways to prepare for a possible tsunami and to avoid one when it happens.

Listen to warnings

Many tsunamis can be detected and their landfall predicted. In places with tsunami warning systems, there may be warnings on the radio or television. Along coasts, sirens may be sounded to warn people to evacuate. Everyone must head for high ground and stay there. People often die after the first wave because they return to their homes too soon or go to the beach to help stranded people or animals, only to be engulfed by another tsunami wave.

Know the signs

In addition to official warnings, natural signs can also indicate that a tsunami is coming. Undersea **earthquakes**, which often cause tsunamis, are often felt on land. Therefore, after an earthquake, it is

In such tsunami risk areas as the Pacific coast in Washington state, signs advise people to leave coastal areas after an earthquake.

TSUNAMI HAZARD ZONE

IN CASE OF EARTHQUAKE, GO TO HIGH GROUND OR INLAND

wise to stay away from the shore. Just before a tsunami arrives, the water along a coastline may retreat far beyond the normal low-tide mark, and ships out at sea may begin to bob up and down violently. In this situation, anyone on the beach should head away from shore and toward the highest ground as fast as possible. People in boats at sea should not return to the harbor if there is a tsunami warning. It is easier for a boat to ride over a tsunami wave in deep water (at least 1,200 feet [370 meters] deep) than in shallower water.

Surviving the surge

What if a tsunami wave is just seconds away and there is no time to climb a hill? The best solution is to go inside a well-constructed building and climb to the highest floor. People have also survived tsunamis by climbing trees and clinging or tying themselves to tree branches with clothing or towels. If caught by a tsunami wave and swept along in the water, do not struggle to swim; this can lead to exhaustion. It is better to grab a floating object if you can and hold on to it, allowing the **current** to carry you.

A satellite image of water quickly receding from a beach in Sri Lanka, just before the 2004 tsunami struck.

TSUNAMI SURVIVAL KIT

In tsunami risk areas, people are encouraged to keep a survival kit in their house or car to take with them if they need to evacuate their area. The kit should include:

- Bottled water
- Long-lasting foods, such as dried fruit, nuts, chocolate, and crackers
- A portable radio
- A map of the area
- Matches in a waterproof container
- Blankets
- A first-aid kit and a supply of essential medicines
- Cash and credit cards
- A flashlight
- Phone numbers of friends

WHAT IS A SEICHE?

Like a tsunami, a seiche *(saysh)* is a type of big wave that can lead to a natural disaster. However, instead of occurring in seas and oceans, seiches *(SAYSH uhz)* are found in enclosed bodies of water, such as lakes or inland seas. Seiches are usually smaller and less harmful than tsunamis.

Lake Superior

Lake Huron

A satellite view of the Great Lakes. Except for Lake Michigan, which lies entirely in the United States, the Great Lakes form a part of the boundary between the United States and Canada.

Lake Michigan

Lake Erie

Lake Ontario

How a seiche works

The word *seiche* is French and means "to sway back and forth." A seiche is a very long wave motion that makes the water in a lake (or other body) move to and fro. First, the water at one side of the lake rises. Then it falls back down, and the water at the other side of the lake is pushed upward. The water keeps rocking back and forth until **friction** against the bottom of the lake gradually causes the seiche to die down.

The type of wave found in a seiche is called a **standing wave**. Instead of rolling across the surface of the water, as an ocean wave does, the water moves up and down on each side of the lake or other body, while the water in the middle stays at the same level.

What causes seiches?

Wind is a common cause of seiches. A strong wind can make the water on one side of a lake start to "pile up." When the wind drops, the water falls back down, and a seiche begins. **Earthquakes**, volcanic **eruptions**, and **landslides** can also cause seiches by making areas of water in a lake move suddenly. Sometimes, tsunamis cause seiches, when water from a tsunami pours into a lake or an enclosed harbor.

Seiche effects

As a seiche wave moves near the shore, it gets higher. As it surges onto the land, it can wash away people, cars, boats, and buildings. Most seiches reach no higher than about 10 feet (3 meters). However, they can still be dangerous, especially if they hit a town or city built on the edge of a large lake. Smaller seiches often snap ships' mooring lines and make boats crash together in harbors.

How a seiche works:
With the standing wave of a seiche, the water rocks back and forth and can surge onto the lake's shores. The water in the middle of the lake stays level. This point is called the wave node.

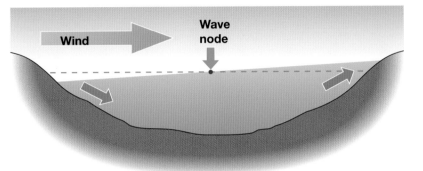

Wind pushes water up on one side of the lake.

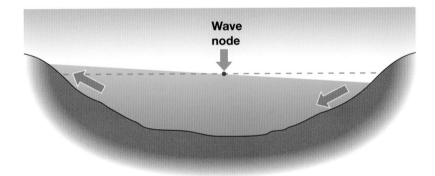

The water falls back down and the water on the other side of the lake rises.

SWIMMING POOL SEICHES

Seiches can happen in small ponds and pools as well as in big lakes—especially after an earthquake. In 1994, the Northridge earthquake shook Los Angeles, California. The vibrations in the ground caused seiches in swimming pools all over southern California as the water in these pools began to sway back and forth and overflow.

**Chicago lies at the southern
end of Lake Michigan.**

THE CHICAGO SEICHE

In 1954, a big seiche on
Lake Michigan struck the city
of Chicago, and people on
the lakefront were caught
by surprise.

Sudden surge

The Chicago seiche struck on a
warm Saturday morning on
June 26, 1954. The city's
beaches and harbors were busy
with swimmers and boaters.
Many had come to enjoy a day's
fishing and were right at the
water's edge, dangling fishing
lines into the lake, when the
surge came. There was no time
for them to run. A wave 10 feet
(3 meters) high swept dozens of
people into the water, and eight
people drowned. Others ran for
safety as the water flooded the
shore, reaching up to 150 feet
(45 meters) inland.

Eyewitness account

On that morning, Ted Sares arrived at Montrose Harbor to go
fishing. He described the effects of the seiche: "As I pulled into the
parking area, I noticed it was full of water despite it being a bright,
sunny day. The lake was unusually choppy. I also noticed people
running toward the pier. There was a sense of something very
serious and bad going on. ... Sunbathers and fishermen were

running for cover. People stumbled and fell. … Among those hurled into the water was Ted Stempinski, who had been fishing with his 16-year-old son, Ralph. Ralph left the beach for a moment just before the wave struck. When he returned, his father was gone."

What caused the seiche?

The Chicago seiche was caused by stormy weather over Lake Michigan. Strong winds and an increase in **atmospheric pressure** pushed down on the water surface, making other areas of the lake rise. As the water moved toward the southern end of the lake, the seiche wave flowed onto the land in Chicago and at several other points along the shore.

THE BUFFALO SEICHE

In 1844, a seiche flooded the city of Buffalo, New York, which lies on the eastern end of Lake Erie. The wave struck at 11 p.m., flowing over a 14-foot (4-meter) seawall and swamping a residential district. About 80 people drowned. Seiches are still common around Buffalo, but in the 1860's, the city built a **breakwater** in the lake, which now protects the city.

The Chicago seiche was caused by stormy weather toward the northern end of Lake Michigan.

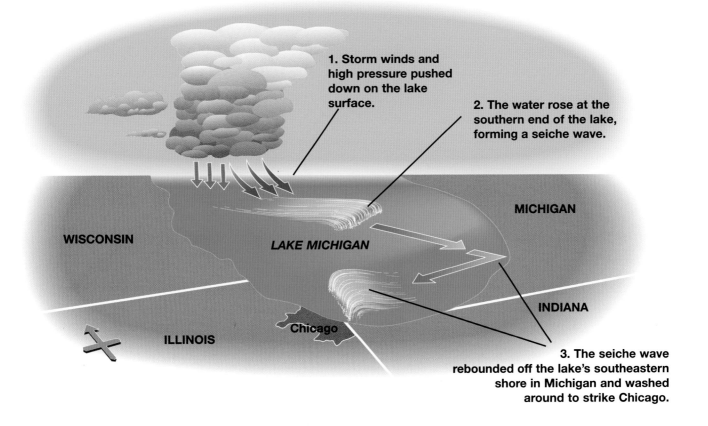

1. Storm winds and high pressure pushed down on the lake surface.

2. The water rose at the southern end of the lake, forming a seiche wave.

MICHIGAN

WISCONSIN

LAKE MICHIGAN

INDIANA

ILLINOIS

Chicago

3. The seiche wave rebounded off the lake's southeastern shore in Michigan and washed around to strike Chicago.

MAKING WAVES

The waves that form seiches can be re-created on a smaller scale using water in a bowl, sink, or bathtub. The water behaves in the same way as in a real lake, forming a small seiche you can watch in action.

A seiche in a pan

As a seiche wave moves up and down a lake, the water level rises and falls at each end, while a point in the middle stays at the same level. You can re-create this wave pattern using a metal baking pan filled with water to represent the lake.

Equipment

- Large, shallow, metal baking pan, rectangular in shape
- Water
- Marker pen or stickers

Instructions

1. Try this standing over a bathtub, or go outside if its warm enough, so any water that spills will not make a mess.

2. Half-fill the pan with water and wait until the water is still and level.

3. Using a marker pen (or a temporary sticker if you don't want to mark the pan), make a mark just above the water level in the center of the long side of the pan.

4. Now turn your hand palm down and place it on the water surface at one end of the pan. Push down through the water gently but firmly several times, about one second apart, to set the water moving.

5. Look at your water-level mark. If you have made a true seiche, the water next to the mark will stay at about the same level while the water level at each end of the pan moves up and down.

The pushing sets up a seiche in the pan. The water moves down first at one end, then at the other.

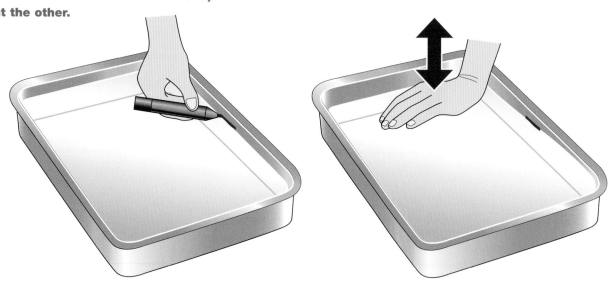

amplitude For waves in water, the distance between the maximum height of a wave and the normal water level.

asteroid A small body made of rock, carbon, or metal that orbits the sun.

atmosphere The layer of gases surrounding Earth.

atmospheric pressure The weight of the air pressing down on Earth's surface.

breakwater A wall or barrier in the water, built to absorb the force of waves, protecting coastal or lakeside settlements.

coral reef A type of underwater environment shaped by limestone formations. Reef limestone consists largely of a framework of skeletons from marine animals called corals.

crater A bowl-shaped hollow in the ground caused by an explosion, an impact, or an underground collapse.

crest The highest point of a wave.

crust The solid outer layer of Earth.

current A flow of water or air in a particular direction.

debris Rubble, broken objects, and other damaged material.

earthquake A shaking of the ground caused by the sudden movement of underground rock.

ejecta Matter ejected, as from a volcano.

epicenter The point on Earth's surface directly above the center (focus) of an earthquake.

eruption The pouring out of gases, lava, and rocks from a volcano.

extinction When all of a species (kind) of living being die out.

fault In geology, a break in Earth's crust.

friction The property that objects have which makes them resist being moved across one another.

geology The study of how Earth formed and how it changes.

gravity The effect of a force of attraction that acts between objects because of their mass—that is, the amount of matter the objects have.

headland A narrow piece of land that juts out into water.

inundation The distance inland (horizontally) reached by a tsunami wave.

landslide A mass of soil and rock that slides down a slope.

lava Molten rock that flows out of a volcano.

local tsunami A tsunami with destructive effects that are limited to coasts near the point of its origin.

megatsunami A very big tsunami, with waves far higher than those of a normal tsunami.

moment magnitude A number used to indicate the strength of an earthquake. Each step on the scale represents a more than thirty-fold increase in the amount of energy released by the earthquake. The largest quake ever recorded, which occurred in the Pacific Ocean near Chile in 1960, had a moment magnitude of 9.5. For earthquakes with a magnitude less than 7, the moment magnitude scale nearly matches the Richter magnitude scale, invented by Charles Richter in 1935. However, moment magnitude measures the strongest earthquakes more accurately.

orbit The path of any object whose motion is controlled by the gravitational pull of another object, such as the path of a planet or asteroid around the sun.

refraction In water, the way waves can change direction as they bend around an obstacle in the water, such as an island.

run up The vertical height above the normal level of the sea reached by water from a tsunami wave as it flows onto the land. The run up can be higher than the tsunami wave itself.

satellite An object that continuously orbits Earth or some other body in space. People use artificial satellites for such tasks as collecting data.

seabed The bottom of the sea or ocean floor.

seismic wave A vibration that travels through Earth, often caused by movement along a fault or a volcanic eruption.

seismograph An instrument that amplifies and records small movements of the ground. From these records, scientists can determine the location and magnitude of earthquakes.

sensor Any one of various devices that detect changes in temperature, radiation, motion, the depth of water, or the like.

sewage Water that contains waste matter produced by human beings. Sewage comes from the sinks and toilets of homes, restaurants, office buildings, and factories. It may include harmful chemicals and disease-producing bacteria.

standing wave A wave characterized by a lack of vibration at certain points. In a seiche, for instance, the water at the center of the lake or other body stays still, while the water at the sides moves up and down.

tectonic plate One of about 30 rigid pieces making up Earth's surface.

tidal gauge An instrument that measures changes in the sea level near coastal areas.

tidal wave A term that was once used to mean a tsunami. The term has fallen out of favor because tsunamis are not related to tides.

tide The rise and fall of water in the ocean caused primarily by variations in the gravitational pull of the moon and sun on different parts of Earth.

transoceanic tsunami (also called a **teletsunami**) A tsunami wave that travels a long distance across an ocean before striking a shore far away from its starting point.

trough The lowest point of a wave.

vaporize To change into vapor (gas.)

volcano An opening in the crust through which ash, gases, and molten rock (lava) from deep underground erupt onto Earth's surface.

wavelength The length of a wave, measured as the distance from one point on a wave (such as the crest) to the same point on the next wave.

wave medium The substance that a wave passes through, such as water.

BOOKS

Krakatau: The Day the World Exploded: August 27, 1883, by Simon Winchester, Harper, 2005

Sweeping Tsunamis, by Richard and Louise Spilsbury, Heinemann, 2005

Tsunami!, by Walter C. Dudley and Min Lee, University of Hawai'i Press, 1998

Tsunami: Hope, Heroes and Incredible Stories of Survival, by Joe Funk (ed.) Triumph Books, 2005

Tsunami Alert!, by Niki Walker, Crabtree, 2006

WEB SITES

http://library.thinkquest.org/04oct/01724/home.html

http://news.bbc.co.uk/1/hi/in_depth/world/2004/asia_quake_disaster/default.stm

http://www.drgeorgepc.com/index.html

http://www.ess.washington.edu/tsunami/index.html

http://www.geo.msu.edu/geo333/seiches.htm

http://www.pbs.org/wnet/savageearth/animations/tsunami/index.html

INDEX